1

The Black Book of the Master Mind - Part 2

By, David K Drews

Disclaimer

The reader is solely responsible for their own personal, financial, business, and life planning decisions. The author is not officially affiliated with any person mentioned in this book.

Introduction

The journey to financial independence and the lifestyle you desire are usually difficult to reach. Financial upheaval has made finding a better job or even paying to fill the gas tank harder. The roots of the financial crisis have only been partially addressed.

Many people look to political leaders, entertainment figures, and various gurus for guidance. If *elites* always told the truth, pretty much everyone would be somewhat better off. Many people look for a way to reach their goals without working, saving, learning skills, investing, studying, researching, being responsible, or by being creative. There are millions who want to place blame or not work or ask for grants from the government. These ideas will not bring financial independence. But the person who learns needed skills, takes calculated risks, and participates in a Master Mind group has a definite advantage.

In a nutshell, I advise you, to start a Master Mind group and really practice what you read or listen to, by, Robert T. Kiyosaki, Anthony Robbins, Dan Kennedy, or your favorite billionaire. Do some of your own research and creative experiments as well.

As I stated in the first Black Book of the Master Mind, keep yourself and your Master Mind closed to outside influences. Be closed to negative influences. Sheeple get jealous. Sheeple are small minded. Sheeple do the same insane stuff every day. Sheeple need to blame others. Sheeple need to be tattle tales to get attention. Sheeple need permission and blessings from their "superiors." There may be astroturfers and other trolls on your Facebook page and groups. There are also those that will switch sides when the going gets rough.

Know for certain it is not a sin to want a better life. If you and your Master Mind group take calculated risks, work hard every day, use your brains, save money, learn what you need to learn, and have a positive yet realistic attitude, you have a good chance. But having the attitude that you will rewrite other people's work and fling it online for affiliate marketers to sell is very lazy thinking. You will likely be accused of being this way before you get a chance to prove yourself. The sheeple just have to bring each other down. Then they cry because no one wants to go to their church.

This book is a collection of thoughts and short writings about Master Mind groups I have written in the year since the first Black Book.

Like the first book, I don't chew your food for you. In this book I mostly explain the challenges prosperity seekers face. It is up to you to decide how to best create the life you want with the help of a Master Mind.

Steering the U.S. Over the Cliff

After the financial crisis of 2008, it became clear that someone wants to steer the U.S. over the cliff. I heard a political science professor say, in 1995, that steering the U.S. over the cliff will make things more equitable for the rest of the world. I had wondered why intercultural communications, majority-minority relations, and a few other topics were pushed so hard by my college. We can see how the U.S. has devolved to crony capitalism and the laws of foreign nations are considered in U.S. courts. We can see the U.S. slowly turn into a third world country. Progressive scholars, teach us that our laws, interests, and safety take a back seat to the interests of the oppressed people of the world. Financial education is hardly taught in U.S. schools. When I asked business majors in school what stocks they liked, they usually said, "I don't know."

The U.S. has as much debt as Gross Domestic Product and the government wants even more revenue. What comes next? My prediction is U.S. and state governments will get more arrogant, more unreasonable, more aggressive and more intrusive before it and its money finally collapse. Be ready for more Taj Mahal schools and other extravagances that our broke government can't afford. Watch for more evil organic farmers to get busted. Watch for kids who rescue woodpeckers to get threatened with jail. Watch for more SWAT teams raiding businesses like Gibson Guitars. Watch for all government and pseudo government agencies to assemble their own SWAT teams. Watch your local GOP duck questions and shuck responsibility. Plan your business and finances accordingly.

See what your Master Mind has to say about the above topic.

Many people will look at the current economic and political environment and declare that it's hopeless. I advise you to cut yourself off from those people if you want to be rich, or if you have a cause or candidate to promote. At least do not let negative beliefs about success become your beliefs. There are things you can do to get rich in this environment. **There are people who survive and thrive in worse environments.**

Cut yourself off from super sheeple who say not to try to get rich and try to scorn you. It's no one's business if you want to get rich. Take action even if phony friends make threats or criticize. **You have to follow your dreams and passions**, not those of some dunce cap wearing sheeple.

I would consider the rise of disruptive technologies in your planning as well. Nanotechnology and robotics can and probably will eventually change the economic landscape as much as the Internet, or air travel, or modern telecommunications. Jobs will likely become even harder to find. I'd find a way to profit from disruptive technologies.

Analysis of Non Entrepreneurial Careers

Getting a job is competitive in part because HR wants people that could compete one day for middle and lower management. Companies will frequently hire people who are way overqualified. Some companies are way better than others. This is an obvious statement, but it is sometimes hard to find out which companies are the good ones. The lines we are told include: seniority means nothing, traditions are always bad, and pay is in line with performance, and on and on. These lines are true some of the time. But basically what it all means is the manufacturing, customer service, and even financial jobs are now overseas and we should get used to being extremely flexible, and underpaid. You and I can receive horrible customer service and then be told we do not have the skills for a job at the same place, when we do. We also know certain people will never be recognized for their dedication, skill, or good conduct.

You can start out in your career being a battering ram for the public. It seems like a lot of jobs these days need people to be intermediaries between some lazy managers and the sometimes angry public. I have had a few jobs where management would not help at all when trouble arose.

If you have a good job, stay put, but don't neglect the saving and investing plans, the side business or your Master Mind. Your company's CEO or your supervisor will eventually retire. You won't be young forever. I would be very suspicious of anyone telling me not to invest for my retirement, especially if I were in my 20's or younger. U.S. companies cannot spew the lines above and then tell you everything will be fine forever. Be wary of Blue Sky Thinking and people who wear rose colored glasses. There are people who want to bring you down. This is not what the establishment wants said right now, but it's true.

Companies sometimes hire other companies to analyze employee behavior in various work situations. When you have a job interview, you might note that the interviewer asks questions that do not apply to you or to the job you are applying for. My best guess is that the interviewing firm is gathering data to sell to other companies who analyze all the data and sell their analysis and conclusions on it.

I had a sales job once where games were played and research was done all the time. It was complete BS. Customers were rare and when we had a customer, the prices would be completely unreasonable. Of course, the managers had the nerve to ask us why we wouldn't really push our customers to pay unrealistic prices. If you decide to start your own business, focus on sales, product creation and market research, not on unnecessary expenses, useless meetings, scams and time wasters.

Many people do not understand productivity means you are maximizing profits while minimizing expenses. Productivity means you are focusing on rewarding tasks, and not wasting time on meetings, lectures, inventing new paperwork, dealing with minutia, etc. If there is one thing that you need to do when you start a business, it's be looking for sales. If you do not avoid or eliminate unnecessary expenses and time wasting, you'll be searching for a job before long. If you have one or more entrepreneur in your Master Mind, ask him or her how they keep expenses low and keep focused on the bottom line.

Too many times, I have heard office workers and service sector employees dress up their pitiful roles, lie about their wages and play inane games. Don't be fooled or sucked into believing the crap you may hear at work, if you have a sh*t job. If your company is going to pay low wages forever, act like it. Lying about how much inevitable opportunity and reward there is at work does not do any good at all. Instead, find out what people, businesses, and government want and may want in the future. Then invest in companies you believe will fill the demand or start your own business and fill the needs of customers with money.

I think it's crazy that the families of politicians and the families of Hollywood can help each other out with their businesses and careers. But at the workplace, this is called favoritism. Most of the sheeple blindly obey and keep each other down. I told you in the first book that breaking away from the crowd takes courage. Join forces with others who want all life has to offer and who are willing to work to get it. Leave the sheeple and start a Master Mind.

Like I said in the first Black Book, it's scary to break from the crowd, but you must do it. Life is far better with a few good individuals as friends, than a hundred phony sheeple friends.

In Biblical times, a person who worked for someone else was called a slave. As the world continues to change and as our rights erode, we can see very clearly that working for someone else is very much like slavery. Hang around with people that are entrepreneurs or that are planning their own ventures.

Recruit One Man Think Tanks

When you are recruiting for your Master Mind, you are trying to catch eagles not turkeys. Don't be afraid to recruit different people. If you read Dr. Gene Landrum, he will tell you that the movers and shakers are different. Look for entrepreneurs who are different in a positive way. Brainwashed people will wait for their favorite talking head, political leader, teacher, or guru to say it's OK to start a business or to invest, or to go to a seminar. Sheeple will wait for all the lights to be green before they make their move. It's amazing how people will claim to be open minded or independent, but then return to the exact same false authorities who offer cookie cutter guidance and advice.

So here's what you do: offer the real deal. Don't hit someone with a cookie cutter. Tell the truth. Talk to people who can think for themselves. Listen to the college student or the small business person who finds profits and puts food on the table. Listen to and recruit serial entrepreneurs or people who have worked directly with them. Walk the talk and hang out with others who walk the talk. Talk with people who read serious books rather than watch dumb on TV.

Don't be afraid of different people. Many of today's billionaires were different people when they were younger. Look at it that way. Many college professors today will ridicule a student who is out of step with the sheeple. Real entrepreneurs don't seek permission to act or think from their accountants, teachers, bosses, or lawyers. (I'm not saying not to consult an excellent lawyer if you need to.) An eccentric entrepreneur does the work and launches a business without worrying about what "they" say. What did Napoleon Hill say about worrying about "they"?

Forget geographic borders too. Entrepreneurs and investors are becoming a lot more common outside the U.S. Billionaires are being made in places like Brazil, Russia, India, and China. Consider inviting foreign people to your network and to your Master Mind. You could find it useful to understand other customs and the ways foreign people think.

Here is one way to recognize a good Master Mind member: he/she will not hang around with people who will not act on attainable goals or attempt to improve their circumstances. Brian Tracy used to say, "push to the front." Pushing to the front is key. Move on your best and most important ideas.

Master Mind groups should remember this quote by Buckminster Fuller, "Innovation is born on the fringe." Don't be afraid of the unknowns you run into. Entrepreneurs may not be what you expect. Many of the most well known, "brilliant" innovators throughout history were "abnormal" by today's standards. But keep in mind there is risk in every venture.

Up and coming entrepreneurs and investors may sleep very little, they might annoy you asking how and why things work the way they do, they might be more loyal and conscientious than big brother would like them to be. They might focus on substance. They might be reluctant to jump on a bandwagon. They might check their facts or use logic. They might be fast moving think tanks. A real individual does not believe they have to be belligerent or petty. Be open-minded. When you see talent or skill, you know it. Be honest with yourself and potential Master Mind members. You will learn valuable things from your Master Mind if you have some non conformists and people with different beliefs and values in it.

If you keep your Master Mind closed, you won't get much backlash from the sheeple.

I heard a podcast by Internet Marketing for Smart People, where Tim Ferris was being interviewed about his book, The Four Hour Work Week. The host of the podcast commented that Ferriss was the learner at a seminar in Las Vegas and not the rock star. There you go. The best-selling author and entrepreneur was taking notes and afterwards, talking to bloggers, getting them to blog about his book. It's the guy with the work ethic that brings home the bacon. The lies at the water cooler bring complacency and the growing of wool.

You have probably heard it said that your income is in proportion to the incomes of your five closest friends. Do you need to change your environment? I figure the average person in the U.S. desperately needs better role models and an environment more conducive to success.

Note: Keep an eye on developments and forecasts affecting your field and make sure you plan for, adapt to, and/or profit from any changes.

Talking Points

Consider the talking points of people you meet. Who do the people you meet sound like? Do they say things are hopeless? Do they sound like communists? Do they sound like a Christian that does not know the Bible very well? Do they sound like a Christian, but constantly imitate some antichristian hero of theirs? Do they sound like a scam artist? Do they sound like they'll be the hand stamper at the pool for 50 years? Is everything they say really vague? Do they make their half truths and vagueness seem like a virtue? Are they in love with the company they work for? Is the person a tattle tale?

Listen to people whose talking points and messages motivate, inspire, or solve a problem. Some people will heap false praise on you, but secretly want to bring you down. You could have seen lows that most people have never seen. Ass hats won't acknowledge this. Ass hats want you to be a good sheeple.

Try to unravel their objectives and beliefs and see if they are compatible with you. Obviously, not everyone has a great future planned for you. People will tell you they love you when they do not. I have had all sorts of bosses, professors, church people, and others try to dictate my beliefs to me and attempt to put me in my place. It doesn't work that way. Quickly ascertain if the person who are talking to is leading you on a path to nowhere (the delay game), or if they are a genuinely nice person. The latter is rarer than you think.

The delay game is probably the most common game complacent types will use against you, in order to keep you in your place, confused, and brainwashed. What we are looking for is honesty.

Treat recruiting for your Master Mind like you would find a spouse. Not everyone is compatible. But you will have to make compromises. You don't want a group member (or a spouse) that answers to "they" and not to you (or even answer to themselves).

Learn about people. Talk to different types of people. Attempt to establish rapport with all people. It's not always possible. See what makes other people tick. Good salesmen, street preachers, and others, all usually have to know a person to see if their organization is the right one for them. Obviously, there are many liars in the world.

Saying what you really think is sometimes the best thing you can do. Lying to people at networking events, at work, and while seeking Master Mind members can lead to headaches. Usually, you can tell the truth and build rapport at the same time. You can sell a lot more by being able to communicate and build rapport with lots of people.

Politics

Don't be afraid to work with people in the other party, if you can. Although it seems like one side wants to end the U.S. and see what's next...thinking they will win out. Recruit people who understand basic economics, are learning skills and are not fooled by the politicians or the talking heads. A kool aid drinker on either side will likely not be able to process information that is different from the ones prescribed from them by the people in D.C. or on TV. I stay away from people on either side who want to strip me of my choices or pre-judge me without knowing me. I also avoid arrogant trolls who act like their whims and fantasies are the will of God. Neither side has anything nice planned for me.

The conservatives are indifferent to the little guy and that brings certain advantages. There is freedom in being self reliant and not being dependent on Big Brother. <u>Entrepreneurship and living life to the full requires us to accept risk, responsibility, and venture out of our comfort zones.</u> Real individuals are pretty rare.

Unite with a small individualistic and goal oriented Master Mind and get to work.

Take your future into your hands. Don't do things that jeopardize your personal or financial freedom. There is a lot of social pressure to put on the dunce cap.

An important question to ask is: how will the next administration or the new congress' policies affect your business and investments? What will the effects be on your competitors? If you know a congressman or a staffer, finding out should be easy. Pay attention to the annual and quarterly reports of the companies you own shares of. Sign up for Google Alerts to keep you abreast of any situation you want to follow. Ask the editor of investment newsletters you subscribe to if there could be significant changes made by a new administration or the next Congress that effect your investments. If you have some great contacts, value them and never mention them around trolls.

The actual wording of new laws are actually far more important than the chants of the paid demonstrators or the talking heads.

Don't be fooled by political games, dirty tricks, smears, manufactured crises, etc. Focus on what the actions of the government mean to you in reality. You might find it useful to learn some of what politicians have to learn. Lots of people will drink the kool aid or be completely asleep to politics. You should answer to yourself and your family and your God, not some political figure or news company. Learn skills that candidates and their staffs know by heart. If you are in a campaign or some other political organization that does not encourage you to learn campaign skills, **drop them like a bad habit**.

A Master Mind could be used to promote a candidate or a cause, if the members chose to do so. Put your heads together and learn the ropes of politics. Like everything else, you will have setbacks. But, if you are organized with others, you have been using mastermind-university dot com, and you have the confidence that comes with having a plan and some money, you could get help furthering your cause.

If you and your Master Mind are going to promote a candidate or cause, you need to learn about the political landscape, especially demographics and the key players in the particular area where you are going to operate. Figure out who your natural enemies and friends are. If you are in a state dominated by the opposing party, I would be careful. I would say nothing to people on the other side about your plans, at least at first. What you do is talk to other activists, including, donors, precinct people, members of think tanks, etc. When I was an undergraduate, I had political opponents, and outright dunces follow me around and play petty games with me. Avoid that whole situation.

At the beginning of your political movement, you want to stay incubated and grow strong. Then you can choose to argue with the other side. Value your friends and allies and respect them. Be careful of the other side creating problems, spreading rumors, and attempting to put you in a "nice" cubby hole.

Watching the news and doing political work are two very different things. One is passive the other is active. One is for sheeple the other for bold individuals. The former is easy and the latter tends to be hard, especially for beginners. People who are activists or candidates have enemies. Watching the news doesn't offend people.

Keep in mind that a lot of people will pose as friends to a certain group and then just waste their time for as long as you let them (the delay game). Many churches and political organizations do this every day. Some people are obviously so sheep-like they will demean, harass, and embarrass their phony friends. I saw a lot of this when I was young. I know some conservatives who do what their progressive pastors tell them to, because they want the recognition, and screw their natural allies and friends over for the other side. Pick a side, burn your bridges. Phony friends are way overrated, despite what anyone dispensing advice on TV or the Internet tells you.

Despite political differences, I am convinced that any Master Mind can function harmoniously if all the members are serious about each other's financial and life goals. Considering how sick society is and how dangerous the Internet and the world can be, I think it safe to be careful when recruiting for your Master Mind offline and online. Use good judgment.

Also, just because the RNC doesn't really resist the campus thought cops and the other nannies doesn't mean you shouldn't. You are responsible for you. The government cannot be responsible for you, unless squalor or a FEMA camp is where you want to live your life. Don't rely on the RNC or the thought cops, rely on yourself. Do not seek approval for your cause or your business from anyone (except maybe your customers or supporters). Join forces with a Master Mind that feel the same way.

Rational Actors & Games

People generally plan their actions with the assumption that the people they come into contact with will be rational. Leaders of all sorts will develop little games where they will create a statement or action for every anticipated rational response the leader or employee may encounter.

31

One problem is, when the desired end result of the plan is a sale of some sort, especially a scam, people will object or become irritated. If deception is used, this can create more problems. No one wants to deal with dishonest salespeople, human resources people, etc.

So here is the solution: think win-win and be honest. When you recruit for your Master Mind or try to make sales, have a way for you and the other person to win, no matter the response. This takes work, but it is well worth it. If your employer or your business is dishonest, this won't work well.

Another game is the delay game. The delay game used to drive me crazy. I had professors, church leaders, my parents, and my employers almost all play the delay game. Basically, to play, you just make statements that put off the other person's desired action for as long as possible. You also need to be able to turn the fault or responsibility of doing the action to the other person. Basically, to play the delay game you lie and tell half truths. You delay as long as possible. You avoid your victim and demonize him and his friends if your victim complains. If possible, help your Master Mind to avoid people that play the delay game. Confront the opposing party if need be. Catch the other side lying if you can.

Be wary of the delay game. When I was young, I knew a kid who wanted to learn to program a computer. (The kid's church said he had to, if he was going to get a good job.) But his Dad wouldn't buy a decent computer, although he easily could, and his Dad usually did anything the church required. His teachers avoided and ignored him, when he asked for computer time. His Dad would say, "What do you learn in scewel?" At school we would just be indoctrinated to be good sheeple. Basically, when you are able, you need to say, "Screw you, I'll do it my way, the right way, the first time." Sheeple will then turn to the rumor mill for revenge or "guidance." When it comes to entrepreneurship, learning to invest and learning any skills, you'll encounter frauds, lazy people, jealous, complacent types, and insane people who think you need to be under their thumb. Live by this motto, "If it's to be, then it's up to me." Cut yourself off from people who disagree. You have no choice.

I have never understood the need for people to bring others down and kill their dreams. I urge my readers to resist those who do. But understand you may be in for a struggle.

Remember, regardless of any games you are in the midst of anywhere, you are good enough. Don't let phony friends and *superiors* suggest you are worthless. It is doubtful that a person could be more than 10-15% smarter than you. They have just as much time in a day and your "superiors" are not actually gods.

If you are trying to join management at work, another business, a clique, or whatever, and you are being delayed or ignored, try a new approach. Argue for yourself. Say "no" to people who try to run you through the mill. Have money for a lawyer and get in good enough physical condition you can fight the douche bag, if that's what his posturing suggests he wants. Start using your spare time productively and start saving and investing. 90%+ of workers will not be promoted to management. But management probably doesn't want you to quit either. Maybe you are a good whipping boy. If you are told you are not good enough, turn it back to the "superior" and ask, "Why don't you help me to be good enough?" Talk things over with your Master Mind and see what solutions you can come up with.

If you are going to have the life and wealth you want, it is up to you. Organizations that claim to help the little guy frequently just want to keep the low wage earning sheeple somewhat happy and occupied. Plenty of churches, pressure groups, "elite" organizations, civic organizations, and the like just want to be sure there are plenty of janitors and sure there is no competition for themselves. It's like they see themselves as Bilderberg enforcers that will share in the spoils when the world is one. Maybe this is why many churches suggest not reading the book of Revelation in the Bible. The pastors and their bosses don't want to hear anti New World Order talk.

People will play games for the sake of playing games. Don't waste your time with these go nowhere types. You have two powerful weapons to use against the gamers: telling them no and mocking them. People who see themselves as elites hate to be mocked and to be told no. Protect yourself by having a cash reserve that will enable you to hire a lawyer. **Seek legal advice from your lawyer and not anyone else! Not anyone!** (Not even your phony friend with all the "social skills.")

Leaders will frequently position themselves to be responsible for successes and not responsible when failures occur. We can all think of leaders like this, but there are vast numbers of leaders (and phony councilors) who get away with scandals. Some leaders even have prestigious organizations give them awards. Don't be fooled.

One game is the blitz. Young people frequently play this game at work. Basically, it goes like this: an ambitious kid gets a low paying job. The kid sucks his boss's ass and reports every little thing possible his coworkers are doing wrong. The kid (who may not know anything about the business) starts making all kinds of requests, demands, and suggestions for improvement. Basically, the kid is trying to earn a livable wage in a job that will never pay one, ever, by acting like a disrespectful kook. If you are going to try this, you need to know what you are doing and be more even keel than the knuckleheads I have seen attempt a blitz. Blitzing a company will not lead to wealth. Blitzing a company leads to frustration. Investing and starting your own business leads to wealth. Avoid people who brag about their huge success blitzing. They are liars.

Be sure to not slack on your savings plan, in case one of these guys shows up. I have a list of money saving ideas at mastermind-university dot com that you need to consider. (I have updated the list since the first book.)

Crazy people account for many of the irrational actors. About 12.2% of the U.S. population is on meds for their minds. When solid plans fail or you are blamed for a national tragedy or one of your employees or master mind group are bawled out for doing something kind, it's probably because of a crazy person (or maybe a crook). Not that your "superior" would care. Narcissistic people are also common and will cause problems too.

Bossing people around when you do not know what you are doing does not work. Instead, ask real, objective experts, people who have done what you are attempting to do. If you want to lead, lead by example. You can only lead by example when you know what you are doing. Leave your ego behind and do the work you must, in order to build your business or get the promotion. You will find building a network much easier by using common sense than attempting to blitz some company somewhere.

Disinformation

It's better to have entrepreneurs, and people in your field, read your work than a professor who hates business, popular writing, or you, personally. I have had professors, phony friends and an assortment of ass hats from all walks of life try to get me off track in several pursuits I have tried.

People will give you false information (BS) when writing, looking for a job, planning the rest of your life, or trying to find the answer to an important question.

But a good source of information, a real one man think tank is indispensable in your Master Mind. For them there is no agenda. There is no political, social, or religious reason to screw with you. The person helps you. You need to be this way in return, too. Your Master Mind should be a valuable asset to all united in your group.

Find out through your Master Mind what works and what does not. There are a lot of things the sales rep at a company won't tell you. They don't have to tell you a one page static site can cost you much, much less than $1000 if you make it yourself. A stockbroker doesn't have to tell you what newsletters or books he reads. When you get the real deal, thank your friend and then use the information.

Bloggers, talking heads, and any corporate person you say could be giving you BS about any fact. They are concerned about their wealth, not yours. A few statistics that matter are: 50% of employees in the U.S. are not happy with their jobs. Up to 17% of Americans live in poverty, while 8.4 million Americans are millionaires. People play fast and loose with statistics. One way to tell when stats are false is when the person reciting them talks real fast and won't let you ask a question about their numbers.

It's amazing the lies you hear when you look for a job, ask for a raise, or chat someplace about careers or investments. Anyway, the important statistic is that most millionaires are or were self employed. No one became a millionaire by acting like a sophomoric jerk at some service sector job. There are many poor people who would hold a piss pot in order to put you in your place.

Some people you talk to in the office and people who talk to you through the TV will all try to build rapport, then, persuade you to listen to their information. Then, they will get you to open your wallet (or retirement accounts) and then maybe start selling for them for free. Persuasion techniques, hypnosis, subliminal messages and covert hypnosis are used by corporations and politicians all the time. If you doubt this, why do think people get excited for candidates, employers, and products that aren't really all that?

Get someone from your Master Mind to demonstrate various hypnosis techniques on you. If there is no one in your group that can, learn to use hypnosis on yourself and others. Then teach your Master Mind what works.

There is a type of hypnosis called the Blitz. What you do is start telling your buddy all the reasons why he can get the job or achieve his goal. You have to really be credible and serious.

Bombard your Master Mind member with his positive attributes and overwhelm his mind with solid reasons to venture out of his comfort zone.

Confidence is a feeling you need to have. Even though you are definitely not evil for wanting to start a business, retire early, further your cause, or reach a worthy goal, many government workers, churches, and media personalities will ask questions that are none of their business, mock you, belittle you, and start rumors. Make sure your confidence is unshakable.

The Goose that Lays the Golden Eggs

Sometimes, people need to leave well enough alone. If you have a business, a job, a stockbroker, or a wife that is worth their weight in gold, leave them be. This is a simple and well reasoned attitude. We hear all the time tradition is bad and change is good. A better way would be good. Only if it's really better. But change for the sake of change? This makes me think of make work projects or businesses with incompetent managers. Make changes that are clearly necessary. Many people think complicated reorganizations, busywork and paperwork are a sign of progress when they are not. I have had many idiots try to get me to spend, invest and waste time on sheer nonsense.

People can reach too far. People can be too ambitious. I'm not saying never to swing for the fences. I'm saying only swing for the fences if you can afford it. Swing for the fences when it makes sense. Some councilors and phony friends represent themselves, not you. Focus on your net worth or net income, not on financial suicide or overextension.

Keep your goose that lays golden eggs. An immature person would kill the goose. Don't blow an inheritance, tax return, or a large bonus. Don't make big customers mad. Don't do real estate deals that make no sense. Don't march up to the president of the company you work for and demand his job. Taking on huge debts is as bad as blowing all your money. Look at law enforcement: does a cop immediately bust a small time drug dealer, or use him to find the big drug dealers? Informants are useful.

In the movie, The Distinguished Gentleman, Eddie Murphy, after cornering some politician says, "Oh, we're gonna rip his balls off!" Speaker Dick Dodge, says, "No, we're going to persuade him." Most people would rip the balls off. That's why most people are broke. If self control is a problem from time to time, talk things over with your Master Mind group. Impulses can be wrong. Advice from phony friends can be devastating.

Share with your Master Mind ways you have kept the goose or geese that provide you with a stream of income. Get ideas about how to keep and enhance the cash that is coming in. This should be one of the first things your Master Mind does, is brainstorm about these gold laying geese.

Fraudulent Financial and Career Councilors

If there is one group of people that has made the lives of average people in the U.S. tougher, it's not politicians, Wall Street, or Hollywood, its fraudulent councilors. These frauds may be H.R. types, or non-licensed councilors, shady investment firm reps, academic councilors, agents, etc. It is very easy to declare yourself an expert and begin advising people to make silly financial and life decisions. Fraudulent councilors frequently receive funding from big corporations in exchange for spreading false messages.

How do you figure out if the person you are talking to is a fraud? Here are several clues I have uncovered before graduating from the School of Hard Knocks. The first are dumb facial expressions. Dumb facial expressions usually indicate a dumb or off script person. Expressions and gestures that have nothing to do with what is being said probably indicate you are talking to a liar.

The fraudulent councilor is not responsible. He needs to get paid. He needs to push his agenda. He'll say in the fine print, "I am not responsible for your losses" and so on. Then the councilor will go on to "guide" you through their information. The fraud will not allow for answers to their attacks and claims, they have a cookie cutter. Everyone is equally worthless in their eyes.

The fraud will likely create a cookie cutter type of template for selling their advice to everyone. They may say their program is custom or personalized, when everyone gets the same thing. The crook may claim you meet special criteria. Or, they could do the opposite and declare you unqualified for a position and try to switch you to the position or product no one wants.

Be careful of blue sky thinking. Who says the job training will lead to a job that pays $100,000 a year? Who says the small cap will increase 50,000%? Who says if you move to a certain town, you'll be rich? If it sounds too good to be true, it probably is. Use math and logic to weigh people's claims. Investigate before you invest. Don't jump into a scam because it's cool or hot or because you'll have big house parties with awesome friends. Look for academic and professional credentials and references. Do background checks on people and businesses when negotiating serious matters. As John Greaney of the Retire Early Home Page says "Sometimes the scam is what's legal."

Recruit Master Mind members that can evaluate stocks, other investments, and the claims made by businesses and people on TV. One man think tanks and armies of one should not have a lot of trouble steering clear of frauds.

Let me give you a few more signs you could be dealing with a fraud. The councilor pretends he can't hear or won't acknowledge. They ask the same questions over and over. They will complain that they want you to be specific or turn around and say don't bog me down with details. When you get the feeling you've been run through the mill, cut your losses.

Psychology

Admit to yourself and your Master Mind what you really want. This makes life within the Master Mind much easier. Be able to explain your biggest four desires in life, at least to yourself. Also, relate your plan for getting there to your Master Mind. A good Master Mind group will probably help you get your real wants faster. Find out what the others in your group want and then you will know how to keep them pressing onward. People's real wants drive them. What we should want doesn't get us very far, according to Tony Robbins.

I am a big believer in following your passions. Tim Ferris suggests his readers do what excites them the most. Ferris also recommends short term goals instead of long term goals, with your short term goals being activities that excite you. This gets more action and productivity out of you. If you haven't read the 4 Hour Work Week, you should, if only for the purpose of practicing lateral thinking.

When you make a decision on your long and short term goals (including non-financial goals) make real decisions. Back up your decisions with action and focused work. Then you may have made a real decision. Tell your Master Mind group about your decision and the plan that backs it. Act upon the feedback you get from your Master Mind with action that you used to make your decision in the first place. Don't waste your group's time. If your Master Mind is of good quality, it will be a good incubator for ideas.

When you and your group have all stated your true goals, it will be easier to reward and motivate them when they make progress. You want to give yourself small rewards for making progress too. People really like to hear kudos and appreciative comments.

NLP is a useful tool for helping us reach our goals. Creating new associations to beliefs, attitudes and behaviors for success are very helpful. Condition yourself to do the most important things. Focus on your vehicle for financial freedom. Then you can help the others in your Master Mind do the same. If you have never read an introductory book on using NLP or have not heard "Get the Edge", by Tony Robbins, you may want to do so.

Rapport is a skill that is useful in pretty much all social and business situations. Like NLP, rapport building is a skill that requires practice to learn. In order to recruit people to your Master Mind, you need some level of rapport. The main things that will help you recruit are:

- Establishing that you have common goals, challenges and enemies.

- With a person completely different from you, relate the ways you and your Master Mind can help them and how they can help you.

- That you have or are working on a plan to buy a private island or to further a cause.

- Put your potential recruit at ease and attempt to inspire confidence.

- Attempt to bring out what the person you are talking to has to offer.

- Demonstrate that you can maintain confidentiality.

Killing Multiple Birds with One Stone

By creating a vision for yourself and your Master Mind you have killed at least two birds with one stone. Having a definite vision gives you a purpose. Having a definite vision means you to have to have goals and plans. Having goals and plans gives you an edge in dealing with people and getting people to follow you, provided you are genuinely determined. You cannot not be aimless if you have a clear and realistic vision and purpose.

With a 401K and a traditional IRA, you have deferred taxes on your investments and you get a write off for your contributions. Plus you have that money invested. That is killing three birds with one stone, if you hold your investments until you retire, if your investments are profitable. But keep in mind taxes on 401K's and Traditional IRA's are higher than the capital gains rate at this time.

By outsourcing some of your work, you free up time to sell and to create new products. (You have to understand the task before you can outsource it.) By having an affiliate program, you have people selling for you. Other marketers may see exactly who to sell your products to. If your product is good and you have enough of a profit margin to share, you can multiply your sales with affiliates.

Where is the Crowd Getting You?

Forget the crowd. Forget what "they" say. Sow the seeds of the things you want to reap, for years if need be. Give and you shall receive! Focus on doing what you need to every day to be successful. Don't let yourself down. Your Master Mind should be good role models. Be grateful if they try to hold you accountable for reaching your goals or participating in the group. That is a big part of what Master Minds are for.

Read every book you know will help you. Practice researching stocks. Play in a stock market tournament. Work out every day. Network at every opportunity. Go do something **you** have always wanted to do. Read something you have always wanted to read. Get some decent casual clothes so you are presentable. Going a little outside your comfort zone every so often helps you grow.

Where has your circle of friends and/or the crowd gotten you? Are you satisfied with your overall situation? If not, start applying things you have read or heard and start to hang out with people smarter and more experienced than you. Remember you are an eagle, not a turkey. Eagles tend to be alone much of the time. You definitely should prefer to be alone, than with sheeple (or a turkey).

Be Selective in Recruiting

Not everyone will be a good fit for your Master Mind. You have to see real determination and seriousness in a prospective member's actions before you let him or her in. Don't become a debate society. Don't become a mental hospital or a worker at juvenile hall. Before you invite a person to your Master Mind, make sure you are not talking to a person who asks permission or approval from some clique or false authority before taking massive or small actions. Keep an eye out for people who have already broken from the crowd or look like they think they should. The latter are the people you want in your Master Mind. Further, you cannot let miscreant trolls anywhere near you or your Master Mind. They are not worth the hassle, even if you can file criminal or civil charges against them.

If you are going to start an offline or online business or begin serious investing, you will get a lot of objections. Sheeple will run off to mommy or teacher or whoever and begin tattle taling. Then rumors will start and con artists will appear. You will get stern warnings from the homely ladies with the confused puppy dog faces that work for the government. Depending on the amount of personal power, cash, and muscle you have, you may have to deal with a bunch of ninnies when you launch your project. Master Minds are great for incubating ideas. You may have to move out of your parent's house, school, dump your spouse or move to a new area to keep the sleaze away.

Monetize Your Passions

There is some debate, currently, whether or not to attempt to start a business doing something you love. If there is demand for the thing you love, I'd say go for it. If you are pro in your field, that will improve your odds of success. If people frequently ask you to make or do something for them, maybe you could sell the product or service. If you are bad at running a business, your passion could turn into a nightmare.

One idea that could really help is to learn all you possibly can about the field your business is in. Learn everything about it, including: how to get potential customers to buy, know what web sites and what TV shows they tend to watch. What are the demographics of most of the customers? Knowing this helps you to identify your target customer. Try to determine where the industry is headed. What external factors affect the industry and your business?

Figure out how to automate your business as much as possible. Have an affiliate program. **Try** to create and sell higher priced items. Whatever you do, divert some of your income into your brokerage accounts. If your business ever fails, and they do all the time, you will have savings to cover your living expenses. Also, there may not be social security for Generation X and Y. So plan accordingly.

There is More to Plan than Vacations

Glorified sheeple love to plan vacations and invent new time consuming paperwork for others. New paperwork is all some dimwits have to offer the world. But, there is a lot more to plan than vacations. Ask yourself the hard questions about how you will provide for yourself and your dependants when you are in your 90's. By asking tough financial questions like this, you will see what you need to do to enjoy life after your working years. More importantly, you will have to think of how to get to that level of wealth and how to preserve that wealth.

A lot of financial councilors and writers will tell their readers to scale their lifestyles way down or to get deep in debt with school loans to increase your income. What I will suggest to you is to find a business you can start that has the potential to make you at least ten million dollars, either in revenue or as a result of the sale of the business. Not that you will know this when you start.

To do this, most of us will start reading the autobiographies of successful business people and learning the nuts and bolts of starting a business. People will scream that this doesn't work and then proceed to offer no alternatives, except to advocate bigger and more irresponsible government. I don't necessarily believe that life is that cold hearted. Learn everything you can that could help you invest better, save money, and launch profitable ventures. Shut out the screams that you can't even hope to be rich from the sheeple. Spend time with your Master Mind, discussing what you read, listen to, see and the **results** you are getting. Go through courses together. Discuss developments in the economy together. Forget there are any naysayers and get to work. Master Minds have to be closed to negative influences. It's amazing what the sheeple and their shepherds will accuse you of.

Something to Plan Right Now

How much will you need to retire? You will eventually need to retire. Figure out how much each of the following expenses cost and add up the total. You want to have investments that will pay all of your expenses. If your job doesn't provide enough to reach your goal, you need to start your own business. Keep the thought of scaling down your lifestyle out of your mind, especially if you already live modestly.

You are going to get the nest egg you need by selling your business and/or investing. You have to shut out the chicken little within. You have to control the child within that wants to blow his wad. You have to ignore the phony friends and *superiors* who say it can't be done.

Your Master Mind group will come in handy if you recruit good quality people. It's a good idea to know people who are smarter and more experienced than you. Listen to the entrepreneurs in your Master Mind, even though this offends some people on TV.

Add up the total of your monthly expenses below. This will give you a target figure for income from investments.

Monthly Expenses:

Rent or mortgage(s)

Health insurance

Vacations and travel

Gas

Start up cost for a new business

Dues

Charity

Hobbies

Gym membership

Seminars, courses, conferences, training

Boat or RV expense

Money for a trading account

Utilities

Assistance for children or parents

Cable TV

Electric

Phone

Other household expenses, including ink cartridges, firewall, etc.

Misc.

Back to Political Causes

An intelligent person will attempt to work the system and think outside the box. (Or own the system.) I wrote an article a few months ago, called,"Beat the Money Game and Retire Early." In that article, I suggest that investors and entrepreneurs support laws that allow citizens to:

1) Opt out of social security

2) Opt out of unemployment insurance (with the majority of saved money going to the worker)

3) Invest in hedge funds

4) Invest in IPO's

Today, I will also add that the capital gains tax should be virtually eliminated and that corporate taxes be as low as other industrialized countries.

Imagine with all these incentives, how hard people would work. Imagine how people would want to invest and start businesses. Imagine how angry the other side would be. Entrepreneurs and investors are evil, according to the socialists. This does not expand the size, scope and reach of government. But, the economy would grow and if the government could be controlled and given therapy, government spending could be reduced and the deficit would be eliminated.

I would guess that 35% of the population of the U.S. would support this legislation. What about the rest? Well, government employees want to see a big and powerful government, not booming commerce. Even though they can print all the money they want, the government wants to keep people poor and under their thumb. More than 35% of the population of the U.S. is registered Republican, but many lack the courage and resolve to act in their own interest and more importantly, avoid the scorn of the *elites*. Many conservative types out here, simply put, don't have the self esteem or self confidence to boldly participate in politics, even online.

My proposal is that those of us who want to grow wealthy push this agenda. The reward could be early retirement or achieving a life-long dream of owning a mansion or whatever. But be wary of traitors, plants, and astroturfers. Lots of people like knowing there is sort of a safety net and many people don't see themselves as either achievers or people who can manage a household. But the above proposals will benefit everyone who works. Even in the 21st century you can't get something for nothing. There are people who call themselves conservatives and listen to Rush Limbaugh every day who do not understand this.

My suggestion is that your Master Mind work, at least a little, to further a pro growth – pro freedom agenda. The socialists will have plenty to say. Be ready for anything. Avoid any person you encounter who twists your words or in any way wastes your time.

Things You Can't Say

Although the economy is shaky, the false elites want to raise taxes even though they can print all the money they want. What is the need to tax more in order to have a few percent more for the government to spend? Why punish achievers? Punishing achievers has never helped the poor or the middle class. The government should instruct its uber sheeple to suggest to their captive audiences that entrepreneurship, investing, and using resources wisely are the way to help the poor and provide enough tax revenue for the greedy people in congress.

Don't waste time watching the news. Spend the time on your business, investments, and personal development. When the government-media complex asks you for your time, I'd tell them no.

Here's something you shouldn't go around saying. Don't compare the modern United States with Weimar Germany. This is a good comparison, though. When Hitler decided to try to take over Germany, some people were excited. Some Germans thought they would get something for nothing, whether it was money or stature. Totalitarianism leads to death. There are many sheeple in the U.S. that are willing to surrender all their rights to the government, in exchange for temporary welfare and every *benefit* that the broke government cannot afford for long.

What's the situation with Social Security right now?

I wouldn't say this either. When Stalin took over Russia, he had his experienced military officers shot. Don't look to a big government to solve your problems. You might basically end up shooting yourself or a friend.

Portland, OR public schools used to teach that everyone is actually a god. The teachers reveled in the brilliance of their students. But how come when a person has a problem with the teachers and their bosses, the former student is called ignorant? I thought they were brilliant gods with a stellar education? How can they be ignorant? Why do brilliant gods need so much attention, scorn and micromanagement from the counterfeit elites?

Here is another great thing not to bring up. You need to learn to invest for yourself. I knew a lady during the Internet bubble. Her dad was a broker. He hung up on people asking to sell their tech mutual funds when the October 2000 Crash happened. Years ago I was interviewed for a job. I told a manager that was studying to be a financial planner that they needed a better 401K. I asked why they used that particular 401k company. The 401K funds were expensive and their performance badly lagged the market. The manager just smiled a silly smile and laughed a silly laugh.

Are you sure you don't want to control your own investments?

Come to find out later on that employers can make money off of their employee's savings plans.

If you decide you need to hire a broker, ask for references. Research the broker and his company at www.sec.gov.

Good writers and good speakers say what everyone is thinking. There are some media personalities who speak for many, and they are paid well.

It is amazing the things we are told. Master Minds can and should share the truth. Get people together who are serious about financial independence and/or advancing their causes. Remember what you hear behind closed doors. Keep your Master Mind closed to negative influences.

Did You Stall and Balk Too Much?

If you stalled and balked too much in your past, admit it to yourself and resolve not to be that way. If you think you need to, ask your Master Mind for assistance with being more of a self starter.

You have heard the stories about the lemmings and how they all run off the cliff together, etc. You have heard and seen how the crowd keeps people down. You have seen (hopefully just on TV) how cults take full control of people's lives. You have heard of racism and other forms of bigotry that attempt to keep people down. I won't tell you any of those stories, but I will tell you to question and to act in your best interest when you know you need to. Be bold and lead by example.

If you attempt to break from the crowd, prepare for judgment from the confused puppy dog people who are **never** judgmental.

Small Teams can be Extremely Effective

A small Master Mind group of average intelligence and resources can kick the ass of a big organization full of geniuses in terms of results, by being proactive and persistently and consistently working on their goals. We read about small companies like that all the time in business magazines.

I have witnessed, here in Oregon, the 3% of republicans that call themselves liberal republicans, are PROACTIVE. They don't ask permission to campaign, volunteer or donate or take classes or go to seminars, or worry about what "they" will say. The libs here brave the flak and press on, proactively. Liberal republicans seem to have a disproportionate say in the party. I have tried to convince more than a few conservatives here in Oregon to go to the Leadership Institute and try a few other proactive ideas. But they usually will not. I believe many conservatives aren't the activists they should be because of fear. I think I have really seen the crowd mentality keeping people quiet, poor, and negative. The Tea

Party has changed this somewhat here in my state, but there is a long way for conservatives to go.

Look at the fraternity Skull and Bones. With maybe 500 living members, they effect change in politics, society and who knows where else. Writer Alexandra Robbins said in her book <u>Secrets of the Tomb</u> that the Bonesmen **all bring something to the table**. That's the approach to have if you dare to defy the ubersheeple. The sidelines won't get you to where you want to be. You need to be proactive and persistent. Killing your TV is a good idea too.

In WWII, small bands of rebels drove the Nazi's crazy. Resistance movements in Europe helped the Allies win. How would you characterize these resistance movements? Hopefully you would call them bold, maybe you would call them proactive. You would probably say they put everything on the line. Watching TV, whining, and spreading gossip isn't gonna help you achieve anything in life.

Are You Really an Executive?

Public schools claim to be raising and training executives. This is pure BS. Judging by the younger people I have worked with over the years, it seems that self education is what matters. Public schools teach their versions of ethics, diversity, and surround math, writing, and history with anti-capitalist and anti-Western thought. Graduates are light on skills, unless they taught themselves or found non-traditional education.

Public schools teach their students to use source documents for their research that are progressive in nature or government documents. Basically, they want you to read the New York Times and more importantly, not to read or cite anything that has non-progressive point of view. I used the Congressional Record as a source once and my dimwit professor fumed at me. These days, I'm sure a videotaped Alex Jones, Bill O'Reilly, or the random blogger's videotaped interviews are all off limits too, even though they are source documents.

This means, if you want to be the executive, you need to teach yourself the skills you need to run your business. Learning programming skills, entrepreneurial skills, cash management skills, small business marketing, market research, SEO, and any other skills you need to be an effective executive, you may have to teach yourself. You were lucky if you were taught practical skills in school.

You cannot be as sloppy and uncaring as the public schools, the government or a large business when it comes to your customers. You have to assume your competitors are working hard to meet their customer's demands. Why should your competitor's customers come to you? You probably do not have a monopoly like the public schools.

Pretty much all governments make promises they cannot keep. You cannot.

In school, you have to ask permission and approval. If you need permission and approval to run your own life after you graduate, you are in trouble.

Since 1993, public colleges have been required to have diversity officers to monitor conservatives, libertarians, Christians, and all other campus groups and protect people from "racism." (How did they know a black socialist would get in the White House in 1993?) Anyway, you need to focus on getting customers and not hiring people to hover over dissidents or whatever you want to call them, in your business.

You and your Master Mind should help each other keep a proper and realistic perspective. The home schooling never ends.

Ask the Tough Questions

You should know that it takes work to create a business that makes money. Do not listen to people online or at seminars who say to just throw a poor product on some dot com and wait for the money to come in. Or just hastily throw a video online and wait for tons of traffic. Quality sells. There is no word of mouth buzz for the inferior product. Affiliate marketers will not even try to sell a terrible product. Be wary of lazy marketers. Also, learn to build a web site yourself. Hiring a web designer is expensive, even if you hire one from overseas.

Avoid recruiting or getting recruited by short sighted people who are after instant success or who ask several times about your total net worth. Ask yourself the tough questions before launching a venture. Here are some questions to get you started:

- Who are my customers?

- Why will people buy from me?

- What is the advantage of my product?

- Do I have the resolve to _____? If I am not really serious will I make things worse if I quit?

- What could I sell to this hungry and growing niche?

- Why do I believe the price of ____ will go up?

- How could I help this person reach their goal?

- Is this a lie someone would tell little children? Is there a better way?

- Why is _____ trying to get me to slack and be irresponsible? Who sent him/her?

- Is this a wise expenditure?

Ask Yourself these Questions

If you are planning a business, you have to do a lot of grunt work. If you want maximum profits, you need to analyze your business and see where you can make improvements. Here is a list of questions to ask yourself about your product or service. The more questions you can answer, the better. If you do not have a business idea, ask yourself these questions and then determine if you can expect to make a product that improves upon an existing product.

Am I duplicating effort?

Can I simplify this task for myself or my customer?

Could I replicate this process?

Is there a better way?

Will this offend anyone? Who? Can I explain away or apologize for this problem?

Why will people buy this from me?

What type of person will like this?

Can this be done cheaper?

Can I improve this?

Where do my competitors advertise?

Which of my customer's buttons should I push?

Who is looking at my site?

Will 100,000 people buy this from me?

How do I build a bridge to _____?

Can I run this business anywhere?

Will I have enough profit margin?

Will I have enough profit margin to pay affiliates a good commission?

If the economy falters, how will my product sell?

Are my expectations realistic? Can I afford to find out?

Am I improving my niche? If so, how much?

Am I using my natural strengths?

Where does this venture lead me?

Can I put the team together to run this business?

Aphorisms of the Master Mind

1

Utopias won't work. Death, fraud and financial catastrophe result from attempting to build real utopias. But a Master Mind group, operating in a spirit of unity and harmony can be a virtual utopia.

2

You can stand up for yourself and speak the truth, at work, in schools, and courtrooms, even if mainstream establishment republicans advise against it. Master Mind groups can and should advocate for each other and an environment conducive to success, rather than a ghetto environment or a command control economy (and society).

3

Unless you have tons of cash, imitating the establishment won't work. Outsourcing, creative abandonment, backgammon, off the books banking deals, delay tactics, cronyism, and an education monopoly have not been good for future generations, entrepreneurs, investors, and liberty and workers in the U.S. (or the world). Who is really looking out for you? Hopefully, your Master Mind and your mentors.

4

Real leaders do not stand idle while their followers are slandered, harassed, or ripped off. Real leaders do not ignore real problems or their follower's interests. Real leaders do not leave their followers hanging in the breeze. There are a lot of poor leaders that pay to have false praise heaped on them. If you become a mentor through a Master Mind group, be responsible. Don't screw up and just hide and screen your calls and talk tough at the bar.

5

Are Christians door mats or not? Christian leaders need to be decisive and consistent.

6

Be as creative as you were when you were six. Ask yourself why you are not as creative as you were back then (unless you are still very creative.) Examine your beliefs about what society, the media, your schools, and your parents taught you about creativity, curiosity, and self reliance. You may need to change some beliefs if you want to really make it big.

7

Here in the U.S., there are lots of people, pretty much everywhere, who will attempt to kill dreams, foil plans, put others down, consolidate their nonexistent powers, and basically argue that they should be at the right had side of God. These people accuse others of being narrow minded, and repeat what they hear from "elites". I have not seen this behavior further a worthy cause, make a person rich, earn a promotion, or lose 60 pounds of body fat. People who are not sheeple or ubershepple need to unite. MasterMinds fit the bill. It's tougher than it sounds. Trolls will eventually find you. Political Correctness will hamper the efforts of those who want to bring the trolls to justice.

8

Your memory needs to be short if you are to be a good sheeple. Your mentors, teachers and bosses most likely influenced your decisions. If you are not happy with where you are, **maybe** you need new advisors. Maybe you need to actually do what your advisors told you. If you think the elites really want to help mankind, watch the movie Endgame on youtube. Think about the 2008 financial crisis and the stimulus program. How about the billions of dollars that went unaccounted for?

9

At my old church one youth pastor said to pray for bad things to happen! The pastor said Lutherans do not have to lose! Which is right? We need to be consistent and not divided against ourselves.

10

I could tell countless stories of "bringing ya down bro" pro-sheeple talk. Instead I will tell you to cut yourself off from the opinions of the elite and their sheeple. Think for yourself. **Analyze your beliefs**. Think about the speech patterns and gestures of people you encounter. Do the exercises Tony Robbins and other success coaches tell you to do and follow through. Don't be lazy. Don't expect immediate gratification. Most talking heads will not like this. Keep your Master Mind closed. Anticipate the scorn, the slander, and desertion by your phony friends. Show appreciation for real Christians and people of other faiths who are honest and practice what they preach.

11

A lot of people are confused about businesses being like the government. Businesses must make a profit. Businesses cannot be run like the government. People lie. Degrees do not guarantee success. How do you know HR is telling you the truth? Who says the salesman is honest? Don't be afraid to question.

12

The elites expect to surrender our rights and money in exchange for taking our burdens. Of course the people on the other side say, "Then we'll have tyranny!"

Here is how the elites try to fool us in school and other public places. They just say they have social skills and won't hurt anyone. They will claim to have faith in a higher power. They tell all kinds of lies. They will build relationships and attempt to project a certain image (with no substance). They want you to have a real short memory. They will divide and conquer the other side, which sometimes won't help itself, each other, or even attempt to keep each other down.

13

Learn skills. Respect natural allies. Meet your allies if possible. Build your mental arsenal. Share your knowledge and resources with your Master Mind. Ignore the verbal attacks of jealous people, trolls, and competitors who want to swipe your tribe, lists, or tarnish your reputation. Create a plan and work the plan diligently. Push to the front. Increase your strength until you are strong enough to make your move. Trolls will offer useless and unconstructive criticism. Be wary. Advance your agenda. People will pose as friends and try to foil your plans. These people are probably total hypocrites. Find out who they answer to. If they say its God, don't believe them, obviously.

If you are successful, reward your Master Mind, and other supporters who helped you.

14

Try to improve the whole lives of your Master Mind, not just the financial. Have the physical health to enjoy your money and freedom. Keep yourself growing. Support a charity you believe in or start one of your own. Volunteer if you can. Be grateful to your God for what you have. This will enhance your spiritual life.

Prevent your Master Mind from getting so big headed they run into trouble with the law or get divorced or fall for a con artist's scheme. Insulate yourself from people who make too big of bets or are reckless with their cash.

15

Think like the producer, not the consumer, MJ DeMarco told us in his book. If you have ever built a web site or ran a business, you know there are tons of people selling you stuff. A lot of the stuff you don't need. You have to control your budget and your time. I am a believer in Dave Ramsey's teaching that one should "act their wage." Definitely make good purchases to improve your life. I would have cash reserves. People who tell you to blow your cash are not your friends. They are jealous. Don't be so desperate to have tons of friends like the people on TV that you spend it all and then get in debt.

Practice self control.

16

Make anchors with your Master Mind. Make your daily life so that when you do, see or say a thing, positive feelings and beliefs come to mind. (Anchoring is an NLP technique.)

If you were to anchor the feeling of self control as far as your budget goes, when you limited your shopping or eating, you felt good about it. If you can really get a few good anchors established, this would help.

Motivation and persistence are topics that Bob and I used to talk about all the time. We would say things like:

- If I can't sleep I will be productive.

- I will mess with this software until I figure it out.

- We will learn stuff and grow while all the sheeple watch TV.

- We will channel our anger and frustration into work and meaningful decisions, while the sheeple blame others, watch TV, drink alcohol, do the same stuff, sleep, make excuses and consult people who keep them complacent.

- We will keep plugging away at our goals after everyone else has given up.

When I am really motivated and productive these kinds of statements will pop into my mind. As you are well aware, we can take "breaks" that go on way too long. A strong anchor should make you snap out of that unproductive state.

What My Master Mind is Like

Since Bob asked me to form a Master Mind with him, I have been taught and seen Internet

Marketing work, like SEO, keyword research, etc. As you can gather from my last book, we share ideas and products that work really well. I write a lot more than the rest of my group. My Master Mind gets the first crack at my writing.

The most important thing my Master Mind teaches and practices is this: <u>don't be complacent</u>. We are not saying never to practice patience. It's just that all the riff raff and go- nowhere types, the average and below average people are complacent. I am not a billionaire, but I am sure the people who do become billionaires, and people who reached worthy goals, were not complacent. Our attitude pretty much comes from Anthony Robbins.

I met one member of my Master Mind in Las Vegas, last year. It's good to have a Las Vegas connection.

I really hope the readers of these Master Mind books will learn and teach their skills and share their experiences with others who need to learn to be an entrepreneur, investor, activist, and who want to learn personal development.

I think it is great you are giving back to your locality and/ or the human race by participating in a motivated and effective Master Mind group.

For further reading:

Rework, by Jason Fried, et al.

Unfair Advantage, by Robert T. Kiyosaki

The Art of War, by Sun Tzu

The Mind Control Manual of Dantalion Jones, by Dantalion Jones

Leadership Secrets of Attila the Hun, by Wess Roberts

Endgame (DVD), by Alex Jones

As a Man Thinketh, James Allen

Secrets of the Tomb, Alexandra Robbins

The Millionaire Messenger, Brandon Burchard

Millionaire Fastlane, MJ DeMarco

Note: My old web site, www.renegadeuniversity.net was somehow destroyed and the hosting company couldn't fix it. I have moved many of the files to a new site:

www.mastermind-university.com

The rest of the files are in the Independent Wealth Yahoo Group. There is also a live chat room at the Yahoo group for recruiting people to your Master Mind.

Also see the following site for updates about Master Mind groups, and future book releases.

http://blackbookofthemastermind.com/index.php